0068512

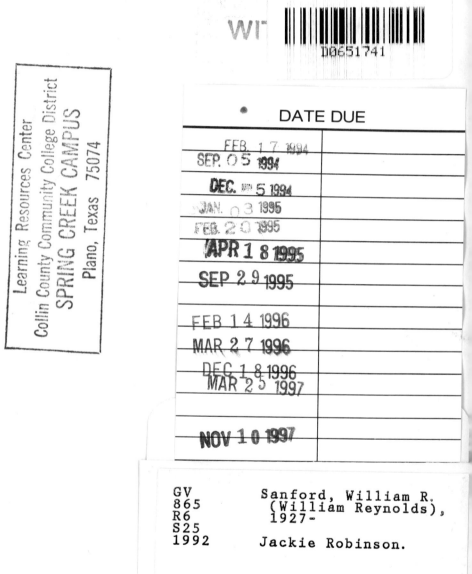

DATE DUE	
FEB. 1 7 1994	
SEP. 0 5 1994	
DEC. 1 5 1994	
JAN. 0 3 1995	
FEB 2 0 1995	
APR 1 8 1995	
SEP 2 9 1995	
FEB 1 4 1996	
MAR 2 7 1996	
DEC 1 8 1996	
MAR 2 5 1997	
NOV 1 0 1997	

JACKIE ROBINSON

by
William R. Sanford
&
Carl R. Green

CRESTWOOD HOUSE
New York

Maxwell Macmillan Canada
Toronto

Maxwell Macmillan International
New York Oxford Singapore Sydney

Library of Congress Cataloging-in-Publication Data
Sanford, William R. (William Reynolds).
  Jackie Robinson / by William R. Sanford and Carl R. Green.
    p. cm. — (Sports immortals)
  Includes bibliographical references (p.).
  Summary: A look at the life of the first Afro-American to play major league baseball, a talented athlete also known as a fighter for equal rights.
  ISBN 0-89686-743-9
  1. Robinson, Jackie, 1919–1972—Juvenile literature. 2. Baseball players—United States—Biography—Juvenile literature. 3. Brooklyn Dodgers (Baseball team)—History—Juvenile literature. [1. Robinson, Jackie, 1919–1972. 2. Baseball players. 3. Afro-Americans—Biography.] I. Green, Carl R. II. Title. III. Series.
GV865.R6S25   1992
796.357'092—dc20
[B]
                                                                                    91-23921

Photo Credits
Cover: The Bettmann Archive
The Bettmann Archive: 4, 7, 8, 11, 12, 22, 26, 28, 29, 30, 33, 34, 37, 39, 43
National Baseball Library, Cooperstown, N.Y.: 13, 15, 17, 18, 21, 24, 27

Macmillan Publishing Company
866 Third Avenue
New York, NY 10022

Maxwell Macmillan Canada, Inc.
1200 Eglinton Avenue East
Suite 200
Don Mills, Ontario M3C 3N1

CRESTWOOD HOUSE

Macmillan Publishing Company is part of the Maxwell Communication Group of Companies.

Produced by Flying Fish Studio

Printed in the United States of America

First edition

10 9 8 7 6 5 4 3 2 1

Contents

NOT AFRAID TO TAKE A CHANCE

Over 50,000 fans jammed Jersey City's Roosevelt Stadium on April 18, 1946. The hometown Giants were opening the **Triple-A** baseball season against the Montreal Royals. By International League standards, the crowd was huge. Many of the fans had come to see the Royals' **rookie** second baseman. Jackie Robinson was playing his first game in organized baseball.

Rookies seldom draw big crowds. Jackie was the exception. He was the first black man to play for a major league farm club. Before 1946 only whites played for **major league** teams.

Branch Rickey, owner of the Brooklyn Dodgers, had given the young athlete his chance. Now Jackie had to prove himself. His hands were sweating when he came up to bat in the first inning. He looked as tense as he felt. The count reached three balls and two strikes. Then he grounded weakly to the shortstop.

Two innings later, Jackie felt more relaxed. With two men on and no outs, he again worked the pitcher to a **full count**. Then, on the next pitch, he swung and hit the ball squarely. It jumped off his bat and sailed over the left field fence. As the fans cheered, Jackie circled the bases with a grin on his face. In the stands, Rachel Robinson shared her husband's joy.

Jackie Robinson having his first tryout for the Montreal Royals

In the fifth inning, Jackie bunted for a base hit. Branch Rickey's words came back to him. "I want you to run those bases like lightning," Rickey had said. "Don't be afraid to take a chance, to steal that extra base." Two pitches later, Jackie did just that. He stole second base and moved to third when the batter grounded out.

Now Jackie put his speed and daring on display. When the pitcher threw to the plate, Jackie dashed halfway down the baseline. The catcher threw to third, but Jackie was there ahead of the ball. During the pitcher's next windup, Jackie again darted down the line. Confused, the pitcher balked. The umpire saw the break in his pitching motion and waved Jackie home.

In the seventh inning, Jackie singled, stole second and scored on a teammate's hit. In the eighth, he cracked his fourth straight hit. After taking third on a single, he danced down the baseline once more. The Giants' relief pitcher lost his rhythm. His **balk** sent Jackie home with another run.

Jackie's four hits led the Royals to a 14–1 win. The black ballplayer had proved that he could play the game. But could he make the jump from Triple-A to the big leagues? Jackie Robinson had been preparing for the challenge for most of his life.

TRIVIA 1*   Jackie was the first black man to play in the major leagues. Who was the second?

* Answers to all Trivia Quiz questions can be found on page 47.

Jackie Robinson reaching for a high ball while working out with the Montreal Royals

7

Jackie catches a ground ball for the Brooklyn Dodgers.

8

A BALLPLAYER GROWS UP

Jack Roosevelt Robinson was born on January 31, 1919, in Cairo, Georgia. Jackie, as Mallie Robinson called her son, was the youngest of five children. His grandfather had been a slave and his father, Jerry, was a **sharecropper**. Jerry Robinson paid half of the crops he raised as rent on his small farm.

The family's fortunes were never bright. They grew worse when Jackie was six months old. Jerry deserted his family and moved to another state. Mallie was left to run the farm by herself. Edgar, the oldest boy, was only ten.

In 1920 Mallie moved her children to Pasadena, California. For a time, she shared a small apartment with her brother Burton. Mallie took in washing to pay her way. Money was always short. Jackie often ate bread dipped in milk and sugar for supper.

Somehow Mallie saved a little money. A welfare agency helped her buy a home on Pepper Street. The white neighbors called the children ugly names and tried to make the Robinsons move. Mallie refused to let the racial taunts drive her away.

The Robinson children were expected to do well in school. Jackie was a fair student, but his heart lay outside the classroom. After school he did odd jobs to make money. He hauled junk, shined shoes and sold newspapers. In his free time, he ran with a

TRIVIA 2

How many positions did Jackie Robinson regularly play during his ten-year major league career?

local gang. The boys were often in trouble. Along with throwing dirt clods at cars, they swiped golf balls. Later the boys sold the balls back to the golfers who had hit them.

Jackie was headed for trouble until two men changed his life. First a mechanic named Carl Anderson took an interest in the boy. As Jackie later wrote, "[Carl] made me see that if I continued with the gang it would hurt my mother as well as myself." Later Karl Downs, a pastor at Jackie's church, became the boy's friend and counselor. He helped channel the boy's energy into sports.

Jackie played all sports—and played them well. His brother Mack says Jackie won the city championship the first time he took up Ping-Pong. Mack was a fine athlete in his own right. In 1936 he finished second to Jesse Owens in the Olympic 200-meter dash. By then Jackie was a four-sport star at Muir Technical High School. He earned letters in football, track, baseball and basketball.

At Pasadena Junior College, Jackie made more headlines. One morning in 1938, he set a long jump record of 25 feet, 6$\frac{1}{2}$ inches. In the afternoon, he changed to his baseball uniform. Playing shortstop he helped his team win the championship. His football and basketball teams also won league titles. College coaches rushed to offer him scholarships.

Jackie chose the University of California at Los Angeles (UCLA). Going to UCLA let him stay close to his family. Football was Jackie's first love in those days. He played halfback and safety on UCLA's unbeaten 1939 team. After the season ended, he moved on to basketball, track and baseball. He played well enough to become UCLA's first four-letter man.

UCLA halfback Jackie Robinson runs with the ball in a game played against Southern California in 1939.

All-around athlete Jackie Robinson competes in a 1940 track meet for UCLA.

In the spring of 1941, Jackie quit school. "A degree will not help me get a good job," he complained to Mallie. He was thinking about marriage to his girlfriend, Rachel Isum. Jackie ended up in Hawaii, working for a builder. On Sundays he played pro football for the Honolulu Bears.

After the season ended, Jackie boarded a ship to sail back to the mainland. On December 7, the news came over the ship's radio: The Japanese had bombed Pearl Harbor.

TIME OUT FOR THE ARMY

Jackie came home to a nation at war. Six months later he received his draft notice. The army sent him to Fort Riley, Kansas, for basic training. While he was there Jackie applied for Officers Candidate School (OCS).

Thanks to Jackie's high test scores, he was picked at once. Then weeks went by while he waited for orders. At last he saw the truth. The army was in no hurry to train black officers.

Jackie Robinson, U.S. Army lieutenant

The long wait ended when Jackie met Joe Louis at Fort Riley. Louis, the world heavyweight boxing champion, had friends in Washington. After the champ made a few phone calls, Jackie's orders came through. He graduated from Fort Riley's OCS in 1943 as a second lieutenant.

The army sent Jackie to a black company as a morale officer. His men were far from happy. They told him that only a few seats were set aside for blacks at the snack bar. When those seats were full, black soldiers had to stand. Jackie pushed hard for change. Thanks to his efforts, more seats were opened up for blacks.

The base commander wanted a winning football team. Because Jackie was an All-American, he was asked to play. All went well until the first game. The University of Missouri sent word it would not play against blacks. All at once, Jackie was given time off to visit his family. He enjoyed the leave, but he knew what lay behind it. When he returned, he quit the team.

In 1944 Jackie was posted at Fort Hood, Texas. The men in his tank unit worked hard for him. As a result, the unit won high marks. That summer an old football injury caused Jackie's ankle to become swollen. He was sent to a nearby hospital to have it checked. While riding on an army bus, he took a seat near the front. The driver told Jackie to move to the rear.

Not long before, the army had ordered an end to seating by race. After Jackie refused to move, the driver reported him. Two

TRIVIA 3

The Dodgers (National League) and the Indians (American League) were the first teams to break the color barrier. Which team in each league was the last?

military policemen took Jackie to their captain. Jackie thought the captain was wrong and told him so. The captain then filed charges against the "uppity" black lieutenant. With the help of his lawyer, Jackie proved that he had not broken any rules. The **court-martial** board found him not guilty.

The trial kept Jackie from going overseas with his unit. By now he was fed up with army life. He asked the army to release him from active duty. In November 1944, his honorable discharge for medical reasons came through.

Jackie took a job coaching basketball at tiny Sam Houston College in Austin, Texas. The all-black school had only 35 male students. In college Jackie had been a fast, aggressive player. Now he coached the same kind of game. His team surprised its fans and enjoyed a winning season.

Coaching was fun, but the pay was poor. Jackie's thoughts turned to pro baseball. He wrote to the Kansas City Monarchs to ask for a tryout. The team's owner knew about Jackie from his days at UCLA. He asked him to join the team for **spring training**.

Jackie makes his way around the bases during spring training.

BRANCH RICKEY GOES OUT ON A LIMB

The Kansas City Monarchs was a Negro League team. If black men wanted to play pro ball, teams like the Monarchs gave them their only opportunities. Stars like Josh Gibson and Cool Papa Bell played for low salaries in the "colored" leagues.

The Monarchs paid Jackie $400 a month to play shortstop. The games were fun, but the travel was tiring. Long bus rides were the rule. On one trip, the team left Kansas City on a Sunday night. The bus drove straight through, reaching the East Coast on Tuesday. The weary Monarchs then played two games that night.

Most of all, Jackie hated the way blacks were treated. Many cities still had **Jim Crow** laws. The Monarchs could not eat in "whites-only" diners and could not sleep in "whites-only" hotels. Jackie and his teammates often ate and slept on the bus.

In New York, one man was planning to break baseball's color barrier. Branch Rickey, owner of the Brooklyn Dodgers, needed good players. He did not care about their race. Rickey recalled a time in 1910 when he had coached at Ohio Wesleyan. On one road trip, a black player named Charley Thomas was denied a hotel room. Rickey arranged for him to sleep on a cot in his own room. That night he vowed to do what he could to end Jim Crow sports.

TRIVIA 4 What was Jackie Robinson's highest batting average as a professional ballplayer?

Jackie negotiates his salary with Branch Rickey, the man responsible for bringing him to major league baseball.

Jackie's speed makes a positive impression on the major league scouts.

In 1945 Rickey thought the time had come. The only things keeping black players off the big league teams were custom and prejudice.

Rickey sent **scouts** to Cuba, Puerto Rico and the Negro Leagues. The scouts thought he was looking for players for a new Negro League team. Rickey's secret plan was to sign a black player for the Dodgers. He knew the man would have to be a great player. More than that, he would have to be a great human being. The first black Dodger would be abused by fans and players alike. He would have to take abuse without letting it affect his play.

The scouts zeroed in on Jackie Robinson. Rickey liked the reports he saw. Jackie was bright and tough. He stood almost six feet tall, weighed 195 pounds and did not drink or smoke. Best of all, he was a slick fielder who could hit with power. As for stealing bases, a scout said, "He runs like a thief."

In August 1945, Rickey asked Jackie to come to his office. When he arrived, Rickey revealed his bold plan to open big league baseball to blacks. The two men talked for three hours.

Rickey was worried about Jackie's temper. As a test, he taunted Jackie with racial insults. He took the parts of a loud-mouthed fan, a redneck teammate and a hostile hotel clerk.

When Rickey finished, Jackie was confused. He asked, "Mr. Rickey, do you want a ballplayer who's afraid to fight back?"

Rickey was ready for that question. "I want a player with guts enough not to fight back," he snapped.

Jackie had been fighting back all his life. Now he saw a chance to open doors for himself and for other blacks. "If you want to take this gamble, I will promise you there will be no incident," Jackie said.

Rickey signed his new ballplayer to a **minor league** contract with the Montreal Royals. Jackie received a $3,500 bonus and $600 a month salary.

STARTING OUT IN MONTREAL

The Dodgers did not announce Jackie's signing for almost two months. When the news broke, it made headlines across the country. Everyone seemed to have an opinion.

Many people were certain that Branch Rickey's plan would fail. Some did not want to see black men playing beside whites. Others claimed that Jackie was not good enough to make it in the big leagues. For the most part, white ballplayers stayed silent.

While the nation buzzed, Jackie was busy. He married Rachel Isum in February 1946. A few weeks later, the couple left for spring training in Florida. The trip was a nightmare. Jackie and Rachel were "bumped" from their plane in New Orleans. The same thing happened in Pensacola. Each time white people took their seats. Jackie and Rachel finished the trip on a bus.

When practice began, reporters asked loaded questions. If Jackie felt angry, he did not show it. "What will you do if one of these pitchers throws at your head?" someone asked. "I'll duck, just like anyone else," Jackie said with a smile.

The rookie did not look good during the first month. By throwing hard to impress his new team, he came up with a sore arm. Then, when Montreal played the Dodgers, his bat failed him. The harder he tried, the worse he played. His critics nodded and said, "I told you so. If he were white they'd have booted him out of camp long ago."

Slowly Jackie learned to relax. The coaches moved him to second base, which was better suited to his arm. He caught on quickly, and his bat came to life. Led by Jackie's hitting and base

Jackie Robinson enters the Dodger dressing room to prepare for a change of uniform as he becomes the first black major league player.

stealing, the Royals got off to a great start. Perhaps some white fans stayed away, but blacks came out in great numbers.

Jackie was tested during every game. In Baltimore there were rumors of race riots. In Indiana a state law forbidding mixed-race sports events kept him on the bench. When the team went to Syracuse, a man held up a black cat. "Hey, Jackie, here's your cousin," he yelled. Jackie let his bat reply for him. In his next at bat, he ripped a double into left field.

Jackie greets his young fans during an exhibition game between Brooklyn and Montreal.

22

At home in Montreal, Jackie was a hero. "Between Montreal and Jackie, it is love at first sight," a reporter said. Jackie and Rachel lived in the French-speaking part of town. When he went out, kids ran after him to ask for his autograph.

Jackie's play silenced the critics. He led the league in batting, and Montreal won the International League **pennant**. The Royals then met the Louisville Colonels in the Little World Series. In Louisville, Jackie had to listen to the worst abuse of his life. He went into a slump, with only one hit in 11 at bats. Montreal lost two games out of three.

Back in Montreal, the fans turned out to cheer their hero. Lifted by the support, Jackie began to hit again. When the last game ended, the fans carried Jackie on their shoulders.

Manager Clay Hopper had once asked Branch Rickey not to send Jackie to Montreal. Now he took his star aside. "You're a great ballplayer and a great gentleman," Hopper said. "It's been wonderful having you on the team."

TRIVIA 5

Jackie was mostly known as a line-drive hitter, yet he could hit with power too. How many home runs did he hit in his career?

THE BIG LEAGUES AT LAST

The Brooklyn Dodgers of 1947 were a strong team. First base was one of the few problems. Fans wondered what Branch Rickey would do to fill the weak spot.

The team trained in Cuba, where the races mixed freely. Rickey was working on his players. He told them that Jackie Robinson could put money in their pockets. If Jackie helped the team win a pennant, Rickey knew, his color would not matter.

Jackie, still with Montreal, hit .625 and stole seven bases against the Dodgers. His fine play did not help. Some of the Dodgers signed a paper saying they would not play with him. Team leaders like Pee Wee Reese and Pete Reiser refused to sign. When he met the players, Rickey threatened to trade anyone who did not tear up the statement. Most of them backed down.

The spring days flew by. Jackie began to think Rickey would never call him up to the big club. Finally, in the early part of April, a storm broke. Happy Chandler, the commissioner of baseball, suspended the Dodger manager. Leo Durocher was too friendly with gamblers, Chandler said. With the sports world's eyes on Leo, Rickey sent out a brief press release. It read, "The Brooklyn Dodgers today purchased the contract of Jackie Robinson from Montreal."

TRIVIA 6 Jackie shares two World Series records. What are they?

Jackie takes a practice swing.

Wearing number 42, Jackie started the season as the Dodger first baseman. On opening day he went 0 for 4. On day two he bunted safely for his first big league hit. In the third game he hammered his first home run. His teammates were coolly polite. Except for Rachel and his young son, Jackie felt very much alone.

The ice began to break in Philadelphia. When Jackie came to bat, the Phillies showered him with abuse. The catcalls and taunts from the players went on and on. Jackie kept his temper in check. He knew he could not fight back. Now, for the first time, his teammates began to stick up for him. The abuse did what Branch Rickey could not do. The Dodgers united behind their black teammate.

Jackie slides into Phil Rizzuto of the New York Yankees during a 1947 World Series game.

The Jackie Robinson family

Support came from many places. The St. Louis Cardinals planned a protest strike, but Ford Frick met them head-on. Frick, the league president, said he would throw the strikers out of baseball. In Boston some players heckled Pee Wee Reese for playing with a black. Reese answered by putting his arm around Jackie's shoulder. In the stands, black fans told one other to ignore racial taunts. Starting fights might spoil Jackie's chances of staying in the big leagues.

Jackie gritted his teeth and kept quiet when opposing players abused him and spiked him. One day second baseman Ed Stanky spoke up. "You yellow-bellied cowards!" he shouted. "Why don't you yell at someone who can answer back?"

Jackie answered the abuse with his bat and his feet. His .297 **batting average** helped the Dodgers win the pennant. The rookie also led the league in stolen bases with 29. In the spring, the *Sporting News* had written that Jackie would flop as a major leaguer. Now the paper named him Rookie of the Year. To honor him, the Dodgers held a Jackie Robinson Day. The fans cheered wildly as he thanked them for his new Cadillac.

The Dodgers lost the World Series to the New York Yankees. That was no disgrace. The Yankees, led by Joe DiMaggio and Yogi Berra, ruled baseball in those years. Later Jackie said the 1947 World Series was "the major thrill of my life."

Jackie is out at second base during this game played against the New York Giants.

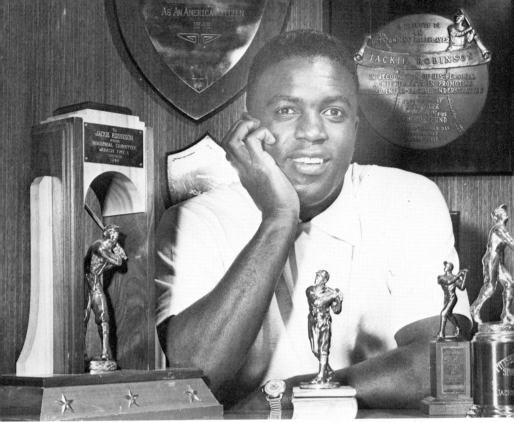

Jackie Robinson surrounded by some of the trophies he won during his baseball career

FIGHTING BACK

The baseball rookie was now a star. During the off-season, Jackie went on tour. He made speeches and picked up awards. His hosts paid him well and fed him well. When Jackie went to spring training in 1948, he was 25 pounds too heavy.

Leo Durocher was back as the Dodgers' manager. He knew that Branch Rickey wanted Jackie at second base. Leo saw the bulging waistline and gave Jackie extra workouts. "Move!" Leo yelled. "There's more lard where you got that. So leave some here."

29

Jackie steals home in a game against the Cubs.

The Dodgers toured the Southwest before the season started. Big crowds came out to see Jackie play. In some cities, blacks had never played against whites before. Jackie did not give the crowds much of a show. He seemed slow and he was not hitting.

Jackie was still in a **slump** when league play began. The Dodgers slowly sank into the cellar. The one bright spot was in the center of the infield. Pee Wee at shortstop and Jackie at second meshed into a great double-play combo. In July Leo left the Dodgers to manage the Giants. By then Jackie had found his batting eye. The Dodgers climbed to third place but could go no higher. Jackie's .296 led the team that year.

By 1949 Jackie had won his place in baseball. Rickey knew that his star's first two years had been painful ones. He told Jackie he could be himself. Rickey also signed two more blacks for the team. Catcher Roy Campanella and pitcher Don Newcombe became stars too.

In shape and much more relaxed, Jackie tore the league apart. He hit with power and ran the bases with speed and daring. At second base, he made tough plays look easy. When the All-Star team was chosen, Jackie was the National League's top vote-getter.

TRIVIA 7

One of Jackie's dreams was to see a black manager in the major leagues. He died three years too soon. Who was the first black manager, and what team hired him?

The pennant race went down to the last day of the season. The Dodgers won, holding their one-game lead. Jackie chalked up a league-leading .342 batting average. He batted in 124 runs and stole 37 bases. Those numbers earned him the honor of being named the league's Most Valuable Player. Only the World Series was a downer. The Dodgers lost to the Yankees in five games.

Jackie was speaking out. When he was not making pitchers nervous with his baserunning, he was taunting them. As a result, he led the league in being hit by the pitcher. Death threats came in the mail. Each time Jackie stood up to the pressure. When he was knocked down, he often came back with a big base hit. In 1950 a letter warned him he would be killed if he played in Cincinnati. Jackie played—and won the game with a home run.

After winning a tight race in 1949, the Dodgers lost one the next year. On the last day of the season, they needed a win over the Phillies to force a play-off. The score was tied, and two men were on base in the ninth. With one out, Jackie came to the plate with his .328 batting average. Knowing that a base hit would win the game, the Phillies walked him. The next two Dodgers flied out, leaving the bases loaded. An inning later, the Phillies won the game and the pennant on a three-run homer.

That winter Jackie starred in a movie about his life. *The Jackie Robinson Story* was a low-budget film, made too quickly. Even so Jackie enjoyed his weeks in Hollywood. It was the calm before another stormy season.

Jackie studies the script for a movie about his life in which he is the star, The Jackie Robinson Story.

Jackie is caught between the catcher and third baseman of the Cubs as he tries to steal home.

THE BEST DODGER TEAM EVER

Branch Rickey left the Dodgers at the end of the 1950 season. Jackie felt as though he were losing a father. Walter O'Malley, the new owner, did not like Jackie's loyalty to Rickey. He also thought that Jackie spoke out too freely.

As Jackie reported it, "That burned me up. I told O'Malley that if he thought I intended to tolerate conditions I had been forced to stand for in the past, he was dead wrong."

Despite his debate with the owner, Jackie had a good year in 1951. In August the Dodgers led the Giants by 13½ games. Day by day, the Giants crept closer. With ten games to play, the lead was down to five games. Blazing hot now, the Giants won all ten. The Dodgers won only four of nine. They had to defeat the Phillies in the final game to force a play-off.

The team traveled to Philadelphia for the game. At the end of nine innings, the score was tied at 8–8. In the twelfth inning, Jackie's "impossible" catch of a line drive saved the tie. Then, two innings later, he clubbed a game-winning home run. Some experts say it was his finest day in baseball.

In the play-offs, the Dodgers and Giants split the first two games. The final game went into the bottom of the ninth with the Dodgers leading 4–1. Somehow, the Giants rallied. Then, with the score 4–2, the Giants' Bobby Thomson blasted a three-run home run.

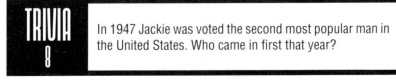

TRIVIA
8

In 1947 Jackie was voted the second most popular man in the United States. Who came in first that year?

Jackie came back in 1952 and batted over .300 for the fourth straight year. His 19 home runs were a career high. At age 33, he could still steal bases—24 of them. The team won a third pennant but lost to the Yankee jinx in the World Series. Jackie was held to only four hits in the seven games.

As usual Jackie spoke out whenever he saw injustice. A few sportswriters said he should be like Roy Campanella. The black catcher did not make speeches about racial matters. He said he was happy to be playing big league ball. Jackie, the critics said, should tend to baseball and make fewer speeches.

Jackie charged the writers like he did catchers who blocked the plate. "If that makes me the kind of guy they can't like, that's tough," he said.

If the 1952 team was strong, the 1953 Dodgers were a powerhouse. The "best Dodger team of all time" won the pennant by 13 games. Jackie batted .329 and drove in 142 runs. Carl Furillo won the batting title. Campanella walked off with his second Most Valuable Player award. In the World Series, Jackie batted .320. That was not enough to turn back the Yankees. The Bronx Bombers won their fifth straight world title.

At home Jackie lived on a busy street with Rachel and his three children. People often knocked on the door and asked to meet him. Finding a better house was not easy. Many New York towns were closed to black families. When Rachel liked a house, it was quickly taken off the market. At last, in 1954, a news report brought the problem to public notice. Jackie and Rachel were soon settled in a new home in Stamford, Connecticut.

Jackie had his home life in order, but the years were catching up to him. His baseball life was drawing to a close.

Jackie reads the comics to his children and his wife as he prepares to retire from baseball.

ROUNDING THIRD AND HEADING FOR HOME

The Dodgers hired a new manager for 1954. O'Malley counted on Walter Alston to guide the team to a World Series win. Alston was a quiet man, as silent as Jackie was noisy. He rarely chatted with his players.

Jackie played hard for Alston but did not respect him. He called the manager a "wooden Indian" who did not back up his players. The conflict grew out of a run-in with an umpire. While Jackie argued a bad call, Alston stood by, never saying a word. Most managers would have tried to protect their player.

Age and leg injuries cut down Jackie's speed. His range in the field was reduced, as was his base stealing. Alston's solution was to move his star to the outfield. A left fielder does not need the quick reactions of a second baseman. When called upon, Jackie also played third base. At the plate, he proved that he could still swing the bat. Jackie hit .311 that year and slammed 15 home runs.

More and more, Jackie thought about quitting. At one point, he started a story for *Look* magazine about leaving baseball. Then he tore it up. He was sure he could still help his team.

Jackie had to fight for playing time in 1955. Although he went to spring training in good shape, Alston kept him on the bench. Jackie complained to a sportswriter. When Alston heard about it, he blew up in front of the team. The two men almost came to blows.

When the season started, the Dodgers won their first ten games. Led by Campanella and Duke Snider, they never looked back. Jackie played left field and third base but appeared in only 105 games. His batting average fell to .256, and he made ten errors.

Jackie later called 1955 his worst year. When World Series time came, the fans forgave him. Late in the first game against the Yankees, Jackie stole home. The Dodgers lost the game, but the daring steal fired up the team. In the seventh game, Johnny Podres ended the long Yankee jinx with a 2–0 shutout. The Brooklyn Dodgers were world champions for the first and only time. Two years later the team moved to Los Angeles.

Most ballplayers say they want to quit while they are still on top. In 1956 Jackie was faced with that choice. No longer a superstar, he was now a part-time player. His hair was turning gray and his legs hurt. He saw action at third base, second base, first base and in the outfield. On the base paths, however, he could still drive pitchers crazy. As one manager said, "If a game lasts long enough, Robinson will find a way to beat you."

Jackie raised his batting average to .275. Better yet, his fiery play inspired his younger teammates. The Dodgers came from

Jackie safely steals home as Yogi Berra, New York Yankee catcher, attempts to tag him out.

behind to win a close three-team race. By winning, they earned the right to play the Yankees in the World Series. It was the team's sixth pennant since Jackie had joined the team.

The series went to seven games after Jackie's clutch base hit won the sixth game. The hit was his last in the major leagues. Jackie went hitless the next day as the Dodgers lost, 9–0. In his final at bat Jackie struck out. Seeing Yogi Berra drop the ball, he ran toward first. Yogi picked up the ball and threw him out. Jackie went out running, just the way he had come in.

TRIVIA 9

Who did the Dodgers trade to make room for Jackie at second base in 1948?

THE FINAL YEARS

In December 1956, Walter O'Malley reached two big decisions. First he made plans to move the Dodgers to Los Angeles. Second, the Dodger owner sold Jackie to the New York Giants. His aging star had always been a thorn in O'Malley's side.

After ten years with the Dodgers, Jackie was shocked by the sale. Could he play for a team he had hated for so long? For their part, the Giants were sure he could help them. They offered Jackie a rich contract and the chance to play next to Willie Mays.

Jackie was tempted, but he said no to the Giants. He had a good job lined up with Chock Full O' Nuts, a restaurant chain. His children were growing up and needed him at home. In a story for *Look*, he wrote, "Pretty soon they're moving you around like a used car. I didn't want that."

Some sports stars are hired by firms for their names and are given little to do. Jackie's job was a real one. One of his tasks was to build up the firm's image. Another was to improve conditions for the blacks who worked for Chock Full O' Nuts. He threw himself into both tasks.

In his spare time, Jackie worked hard for black causes. Because of his fame, people listened when he spoke. He traveled and raised money for the **NAACP**. In 1964 he helped set up the Freedom National Bank in New York City. The black-owned bank made the loans to blacks that white bankers would not make.

In 1960 the men running for president asked for Jackie's help. After meeting with Senator John Kennedy and Vice President Richard Nixon, Jackie backed Nixon. He thought the Republican had more forceful views on racial problems. Despite Jackie's support, many blacks voted against Nixon. Kennedy won by a whisker.

Four years later, Jackie left his job to work for Nelson Rockefeller. The Republican governor wanted to run for the White House. After Rockefeller lost his bid, some blacks called Jackie an Uncle Tom. The Democratic party, they said, was the only party that helped blacks. Jackie fired back. He said that blacks needed friends in both parties.

Jackie turned 50 in 1969. He looked much older. His hair was snow-white. Diabetes had dimmed his eyesight. His heart was giving him trouble, and he walked with a limp. Bad news seemed to haunt him. First Branch Rickey died, and then his mother. Jackie, Jr., came home from Vietnam with a drug habit. With his parents' help, Jackie, Jr., entered a program for drug users. The program turned the young man's life around. He helped other drug users until he died in a car accident in 1971.

In June of 1972, Jackie enjoyed a final moment of glory. The Los Angeles Dodgers held a special day for him. Jackie watched with pride as the team retired uniform number 42. He had first worn that number 25 years earlier in Brooklyn.

In October Jackie threw out the first ball of the second game of the World Series. Nine days later he died of a heart attack. Many of his old teammates came to the funeral to say good-bye. The Reverend Jesse Jackson spoke to the mourners. He told them, "In his last dash, Jackie stole home and Jackie is safe."

TRIVIA 10	Jackie played in 38 World Series games as a Dodger. Who holds the record for playing in the most World Series games?

41

JACKIE ROBINSON, BASEBALL IMMORTAL

Jackie Robinson will not be forgotten. His battle to break baseball's color barrier was enough to earn him a place in history. But Jackie was more than a fighter for equal rights. He was a gifted ballplayer. His .311 lifetime batting average and his fielding records prove that. With Jackie leading the way, the Dodgers won pennants and a World Series.

The awards he won serve as vivid reminders of his talent. Jackie played in six All-Star games. He was a Rookie of the Year (1947) and the league's Most Valuable Player (1949). Since 1987 the Rookie of the Year award has been named for him. In 1962 the Baseball Writers Association of America voted Jackie into the National Baseball Hall of Fame. He was the first black chosen for baseball's highest honor.

Today blacks are key members of all big league baseball teams. Some of the younger players do not know what Jackie did for them. In 1986 Vince Coleman, then a star for the St. Louis Cardinals, was asked about Jackie. "I don't know nothing about no Jackie Robinson," Coleman said.

Joe Black, one of Jackie's teammates, sent Coleman a letter. "It hurt me to read that," Black wrote. "Are black athletes so blinded . . . that they fail to remember that someone had to 'open the doors'? . . . Vince, Jackie Robinson was more than an athlete. He was a man. He stood alone as he challenged and integrated major league baseball. His task was not easy or quick. He suffered many physical and mental hurts. He accepted and overcame the slings, slams and insults so that black youths, such as you, could dream of playing major league baseball."

Jackie Robinson (left) *and the Reverend Martin Luther King, Jr., receive honorary degrees at Howard University's 1957 commencement exercises.*

Outside of baseball, Jackie worked hard for the **civil rights** movement. He admired Martin Luther King, Jr., but did not always agree with his methods. That did not bother the black leader. King was quick to pay tribute to Jackie. "You will never know how easy it was for me because of Jackie Robinson," he said.

The nation Jackie helped awaken to racial injustice has also paid tribute. His life was dramatized in a Broadway musical called *The First*. In 1982 the post office also honored Jackie Robinson. He became the first baseball player to appear on a U.S. postage stamp.

In 1990 *Life* magazine printed a list of the century's most important Americans. Only two baseball players made the list— Babe Ruth and Jackie Robinson. As one writer said, "Babe Ruth changed baseball; Jackie Robinson changed America."

43

GLOSSARY

balk—An illegal motion made by a pitcher during the windup. When a balk is called, base runners advance one base, and a ball is called on the batter.

batting average—A measure of a batter's success at the plate. Batting averages are figured by dividing the number of hits by the times at bat. Thus someone who collects 35 hits in 100 at bats would have a batting average of .350.

civil rights—The rights guaranteed to all citizens of the United States by the U.S. Constitution.

court-martial—A trial by a military court.

full count—When the pitcher has a count of three balls and two strikes on the batter.

Jim Crow—A name given to laws and customs that once were used to keep blacks separate from whites.

major league—The highest level of organized baseball. Only teams belonging to the National and American leagues can be called major league.

minor leagues—The lower levels of organized baseball. Most players begin their careers in the minors. Only the best players work their way up to the major league.

NAACP (National Association for the Advancement of Colored People)—An organization that works to win equal rights for black people in the United States.

pennant—A team that "wins a pennant" has won its league championship. Pennant winners go on to play in the World Series.

rookie—A ballplayer who is playing in the majors for the first time.

scout—Someone who checks out young ballplayers to see if they have what it takes to play professional baseball.

sharecroppers—Poor families who pay the rent on their farms by giving part of their crops to the landowner.

slump—A time during the season when everything seems to go wrong for a ballplayer. Batters in a slump cannot get their usual number of hits, no matter how hard they try.

spring training—The weeks during which teams send their players to warm-weather states to prepare for the coming season.

Triple-A—The highest level of minor league baseball.

MORE GOOD READING ABOUT JACKIE ROBINSON

Allen, Maury. *Jackie Robinson: A Life Remembered*. New York: Franklin Watts, 1987.

Frommer, Harvey. *Rickey and Robinson: The Men Who Broke Baseball's Color Barrier*. New York: Macmillan Publishing Co., 1982.

Holmes, Tommy. *The Dodgers*. New York: Macmillan Publishing Co., 1975.

Robinson, Jackie (as told to Alfred Duckett). *I Never Had It Made*. New York: G. P. Putnam's Sons, 1972.

Scott, Richard. *Jackie Robinson*. New York: Chelsea House Publishers, 1987.

Shapiro, Milton J. *Jackie Robinson of the Brooklyn Dodgers*. New York: Julian Messner, 1965.

Tygiel, Jules. *Baseball's Great Experiment: Jackie Robinson and His Legacy*. New York: Oxford University Press, 1983.

JACKIE ROBINSON TRIVIA QUIZ

1: Larry Doby pinch-hit for the Cleveland Indians on July 5, 1947. He played his first full game the next day.

2: Jackie regularly played four positions—first base, second base, third base and left field.

3: The Philadelphia Phillies (1957) was the last team in the National League to sign a black ballplayer. The Boston Red Sox (1959) was the last team in the American League.

4: In 1946 Jackie hit .349 at Montreal. His best year in the major leagues was 1949, when he hit .342.

5: Jackie hit 137 home runs in his ten-year major league career. Because of his ability to drive in runs, he often hit cleanup (fourth in the Dodgers' batting order).

6: In the 1952 series, Jackie walked four times in a single game, tying a record held by four other players. In 1955 he became one of 12 players who have stolen home in a World Series game.

7: The Cleveland Indians hired Frank Robinson as their manager in 1975.

8: Singer and film star Bing Crosby was voted the most popular man in the United States in 1947. Coming in second to the popular Crosby was a good measure of Jackie's impact on this country.

9: The Dodgers traded second baseman Eddie Stanky in 1948. Jackie was Stanky's equal on defense and a much better hitter.

10: Yogi Berra, the great Yankee catcher, played in 75 World Series games from 1947 to 1963.

INDEX

48